Wolfgang Amadeo Mozart Mozart

TELL ME ABOUT COMPOSERS

WOLFGANG AMADEUS MOZART

written by
John Malam

Evans

Evans Brothers Limited

Wolfgango Amadeo Mozart   *Wolfgango Amadeo Mozart*

Published by Evans Brothers Limited
2A Portman Mansions
Chiltern Street
London W1M 1LE

© Evans Brothers Limited 1997

First published 1997

Printed by Graficas Reunidas SA, Spain

ISBN 0 237 51723 X

British Library Cataloguing in Publication data.
A catalogue record for this book is available from
the British Library.

Wolfgang Amadeus Mozart was born in Austria nearly 250 years ago. He had a gift for writing music, and he became a composer. People from all over Europe listened to his music. He was famous everywhere. Sadly, Wolfgang only had a short life. He died a poor, young man. This is his story.

Mozart, aged fourteen. He is wearing a wig over his own hair. People wore wigs to look smart.

Wolfgang's parents were Leopold and Anna Maria. They had seven children. Five children died. Wolfgang was born in 1756. Only Wolfgang and his sister, Maria Anna, survived and grew up.

Wolfgang's sister was four years older than he was. He called her Nannerl, which was a friendly nickname.

Wolfgang and his sister, Nannerl

The house in Salzburg, Austria, where Mozart was born. Today it is a museum.

6

Wolfgang Amadea Mozart *Wolfgang Amadea Mozart*

Wolfgang was born into a world of music. His father played the violin in the archbishop's orchestra and he wrote music too.

When Wolfgang was three, he listened to Nannerl playing the harpsichord. He tried to play it, too, listening for notes that sounded good together.

Wolfgang's father, Leopold

The house where young Mozart lived. He played on this clavichord, which is like a piano. He played the violin too.

Leopold taught Wolfgang everything he could about music. Wolfgang could write music before he could write words. Leopold was proud of both his children, and he wanted people to know about them. This meant the family had to travel.

First they went to Vienna, a big city in Austria. It took five days by horse and coach to get there. In Vienna, they played for the royal family.

In Vienna, Wolfgang played to the Emperor and Empress.

The Emperor called Wolfgang a "little wizard". The Empress gave Wolfgang and Nannerl expensive clothes.

In London, Wolfgang and Nannerl played for the King and Queen. The family liked London, and stayed for more than a year.

Wolfgang and Nannerl wearing the clothes the Empress of Austria gave them.

9

Wolfgang was a child wonder. By the age of twelve he had written an opera, and many other pieces of music. Some musicians became jealous. They said Wolfgang was too young to have written such wonderful music. They would not play it.

Sometimes people ate and chatted while Wolfgang played. He did not like playing to people who did not listen properly.

Mozart wrote this music in an exercise book when he was eight years old.

When Wolfgang was twenty-three he took a job in the archbishop's orchestra, playing the organ. He was unhappy and felt he was treated like a servant. One day Wolfgang and the archbishop had an argument, and Wolfgang had to leave the orchestra.

Salzburg, where Mozart worked for the archbishop. He played the organ in the cathedral.

Wolfgang went to Vienna, where he fell in love with Constanze Weber. She was a singer. They married and moved into a big flat. Then a sad thing happened. Shortly after their first baby was born, they went to visit Wolfgang's father. They left the baby boy with his nanny. While they were away, the baby died.

Constanze, Mozart's wife

Wolfgang and Constanze had five more children. Only two boys, Karl and Franz, survived. All their other children died.

Wolfgang and Constanze were always short of money. They bought fine clothes and held parties for their friends. They even had their own carriage, which was a great luxury in those days.

Mozart's children, Karl and Franz

13

Soon, Wolfgang and Constanze could not afford to keep their big flat. They moved to a smaller flat, and then to another. Wolfgang wrote letters, asking friends for money.

Wolfgang carried on writing music. Some of his best pieces were written at the hardest time of his life. One of Wolfgang's greatest operas was "The Marriage of Figaro". It tells the story of a man and woman and how they try to get married. Audiences loved it, and sang its songs.

A building in Vienna where Mozart and Constanze had a flat.

In between writing operas, Wolfgang wrote music for stringed instruments and pianos. He taught music students and played to audiences. He worked hard and was always busy, but he did not earn much money.

"The Marriage of Figaro" is still a favourite opera.

People all over the world listen to Mozart's operas in opera houses, like this one in Italy.

Wolfgang Amadeo Mozart   Wolfgang Amadeo Mozart

In the last year of his life, he wrote "The Magic Flute", which was more like a pantomime than an opera. It tells the story of how a magician rescues a princess from her wicked mother. It was an instant success. He also wrote a Requiem, music that is played for a dead person. Another composer wanted to pretend he had written it, but Constanze found out the truth.

A performance of Mozart's Requiem, in a church in Austria.

Wolfgang had become very ill. He fainted a lot and had stomach pains. He thought his enemies had poisoned him, but this was not true. His kidneys were weak and his doctors could do nothing to save him. He died on the 5th of December, 1791. He was thirty-five years old.

Mozart kept on writing music even when he was very ill.

Wolfgang had died poor and there was no money for Constanze to pay for a good funeral. The great composer was wrapped in a sack and buried in an unmarked grave.

It was a sad end to a great life. In his short life he wrote more than 600 pieces of music.

Wolfgang Amadeus Mozart was a "pop star" of his time. It was said that "the magic of his music lights the darkness of people's lives".

No one knows where Mozart is buried. This memorial is in Vienna. The broken column shows that Mozart's life was cut short.

W A
MOZART

1756-1791

In 1996 a great discovery was made in America. Part of a song written by Wolfgang was found hidden in an attic. No one knows how it got there. Everyone was very excited to hear the song. It was the first time it had been heard for more than two hundred years.

The music that was found in an attic

The part of the song that was found only takes one minute to sing. The rest is still missing.

19

Important dates

1756 Wolfgang Amadeus Mozart was born in Salzburg, Austria

1759 Age 3 – he began to play the harpsichord

1762 Age 6 – he wrote his first pieces of music; he went on his first tour to play music

1764 Age 8 – the family lived in London

1765 Age 9 – he wrote his first symphony

1769 Age 13 – his father took him to Italy; his first opera was performed

1777 Age 21 – he went to Paris

1778 Age 22 – his mother died

1779 Age 23 – he joined the Archbishop of Salzburg's orchestra

1781 Age 25 – he left the Archbishop of Salzburg's orchestra

1782 Age 26 – he married Constanze Weber

1784 Age 28 – his son, Karl, was born

1786 Age 30 – he wrote the opera "The Marriage of Figaro"

1787 Age 31 – his father died

1791 Age 35 – he wrote the opera "The Magic Flute"; his son, Franz, was born; Wolfgang Amadeus Mozart died in Vienna

1842 Constanze died, aged 80

20

Keywords

clavichord
a musical instrument with a keyboard. It has metal strings which are hit

composer
someone who writes music for other people to play

harpsichord
a musical instrument with a keyboard. It has metal strings which are plucked

opera
a play set to music where actors and actresses have songs to sing

orchestra
a group of musicians who play the music written by a composer

symphony
a piece of music written for a whole orchestra to play, not just one instrument

A statue of Mozart in Salzburg

Index